Struck

Down

but Not

Destroyed

Revised Edition

Dr. Maureen I. Austin

Struck Down but Not Destroyed
Copyright: © 2015 Dr. Maureen I. Austin
Email: ralphmau@yahoo.com

First Published by Lacepoint Publishing 2014

All rights reserved under international Copyright Law. This Book is a seed into the Kingdom of God. Hence contents may be reproduced in whole or in part in any form for non-profit use without the written consent of the Author, as long as such actions are guarded by integrity, honour and proper accreditation.

Revised Edition Published by Chiysonovelty International 2015

ISBN: 9785317641
ISBN-13: 978-978-53176-4-0

Chiysonovelty International
Plot 8 Evule Avenue
Aba,
Nigeria
Email: chiyson@minister.com
Phone: 234-818-118-3131

Printed in the United States of America

All Scripture, unless otherwise stated, are taken from the New King James Version of the Bible. Copyright 1979, 1980, 1982, 1990, Thomas Nelson Inc.

The views expressed in this work are solely those of the author and do not necessarily reflect the views of the Publisher, and the Publisher hereby disclaims any responsibility for them.

To God Be the Glory, Great Things He has done.

FOREWORD

This book is simply extraordinary. It has been a privilege to read *"Struck Down but Not Destroyed"* in manuscript. Here is a book with which I thoroughly agree and which I can heartily endorse without reservation.

The title is challenging and the treatment convincing. As you read the book, you soon discover that it is not the vaporizing of novice ambitions to become an Author; but rather the product of firm convictions based upon a careful searching of the scriptures, matured by meditation and strengthened by what the writer had gone through. This must be largely due to the way God has wired Maureen as demonstrated through her personal stories and experiences.

This book is about how to be satisfied in God that the power of His joy is released *"to love people better in the midst of a very challenging circumstance."* I am happy to entice all kinds of people to this book. There are surprising tastes everywhere. Like; *"I was only a child yet every night I wet my pillows with tears, pondering within me if this happens in every home...." I learnt to question God at an early age and doubting His love towards...."As a child I watched my mother being beaten, battered, abused, stripped naked and covered in her own pool of blood yet without lifting a finger to fight back...." "My father constantly told me that I would amount to nobody just for attending church with my Mum..." I often wondered why God allowed me to be raised in such a dysfunctional family...." "But the sequence of events occurring in my life and family pushed me deeper to search the scriptures."*

May God give this book wings for the glory of Christ and for the good of mankind; and may it bring a blessing back to the Author with wholeness and joy in every area of her life, Amen.

Pastor Sogo Adelaja,
The Redeemed Christian Church of God,
Hope of Glory parish County Dublin,
Republic of Ireland

CONTENTS

	Foreword	IV
	Acknowledgments	VII
	Introduction	1
1	The Journey of Life	Pg #3
2	Life as a Dream	Pg #11
3	Your Perspective of Life	Pg #21
4	Power of Confession	Pg #27
5	The Propelling Force	Pg #40
6	Flee at All Cost	Pg #53
7	Power of Forgiveness	Pg #64
8	Looking Unto Jesus	Pg #74
9	God's Grace, Your Gain	Pg #80
	Conclusion	Pg #88
	About the Author	Pg #93
	About the Book	Pg #94

ACKNOWLEDGMENTS

I give glory and honour to the Lord for the privilege and grace to undertake this service.

I am grateful for the encouragement and support of my beloved mummy (*Mrs. Elizabeth Ejiaka Festus*) who stood by me against all odds constantly lifting me up in the place of prayer, and her wonderful words of wisdom that brought me this far.

To my mentor and shepherd pastor Solomon Olu'sogo Adelaja and his outstanding wife Abiodun Adelaja who prayed, encouraged and directed me in the counsel of the Lord through the darkest period of my life, always willing to put smiles on my face, God Almighty will repay you beyond measures.

To my friend, my sister, my confidant, my beloved Ojuolape Esther Emmanuel, thank you for your shoulders that became my stay, you're indeed a great friend and a source of inspiration.

To my daughter, my princess, my angel, Dorine Amarachukwu, you are a jewel, a precious gift from Jehovah to me, God bless you for those smiles you brought my way.

To Pastor Abiola & Deaconess Precious Ganiyu, you are a rare gem; to my friend Ms Ethel Lawrence, you're a friend indeed.

To my siblings you're indeed a wonderful people. To the family of the Redeemed Christian Church of God, Hope of glory parish, a family united by the love of God. You are blessed indeed.

INTRODUCTION

"In the beginning God created the heaven and the earth."
(Genesis 1:1)

The creation of the universe showcases the Almightiness of God; His wonderful works displays His awesomeness. We are pencils in God's hands and He daily renews us to bring out the best from within us.

"But now o lord, you are our father, we are the clay and you our potter, and all we are the work of your hand."
(Isaiah 64:8 NKJV)

The beauty of man's existence is that God planned our lives even before our creation and He took an extra time to make man in His own image.

No wonder the psalmist acknowledge this in **Psalm 139:14 (KJV)** *"I will praise thee; for I am wonderfully made: marvelous are thy works and that my soul knoweth right well."*

So when situations aren't working out fine the way you envisaged, when storms of life rages against you, remember that God's unseen hand is busy refining His product. His assurance to those that believe will never be aborted. God is able to perfect that which concerns you.

"Yea though I walk through the valley of the shadow of death, I will fear no evil; for thou art with me thy rod and thy staff they comfort me." (**Psalm 23:4 KJV**)

God is working from the inside to bring out the gold within. Is your life in shambles? The potter is here to put you back together again…let the master artist beautify your life and showcase the gold within.

CHAPTER ONE

THE JOURNEY OF LIFE

"For I know the thoughts I think towards you saith the lord, thoughts of peace and not of evil, to give you an expected end ..." (**Jeremiah 29:11 KJV**)

Life is a journey often times filled with problems and challenges that leaves one in a state of dilemma, hardship, heartaches, broken heartedness and intermittent joy and celebration.

These challenges will test our courage, strength and faith in God. No matter the obstacles we stumble upon as we journey through life, God's grace is always available and it's sufficient too.

Many times we find ourselves in the battle fields of life surrounded by self-doubt, pain and tragedy. In moment like these, our assurance of faith in God is the only weapon that grants us victory.

Personally I had been in situations where I thought God had abandoned me, I had been struck down, broken but not destroyed because God has been faithful in fulfilling his words concerning me.

"Yea though I walk through the valley of shadow of death, I will fear no evil, for thou art with me, thy rod and thy staff they comfort me…" (**Psalm 23:4 KJV**)

I was born like every other child but found myself in a dysfunctional family where abuse was considered normal, blood seen as water on daily basis, crying was my outlet and considered as a normal way of life, I was only a child yet every night I wet my pillows with tears, pondering within me if this happens in every home.

I learnt to question God at an early age and doubting his love towards me because of the things I passed through at the tender age. I often dread the breaking of a new day for fear of the unknown, wondering what the event and drama of the day would be.

I always felt better and happier when I was away from home, if only for the moment of peace I would enjoy before returning back to the jungle I called home.

Gradually bitterness eroded my life, I saw nothing good in my father and this affected my relationship with him and my sense of judgment too. On several occasions I wished I could hurt him badly and end this misery but I couldn't because of my Mum.

My mother was persecuted abused, maltreated because she chose to serve God. *"What a resilient woman"*, she made up her mind to train her children in the way of the Lord regardless of what she was passing through.

"Train up a child in a way he should go and when he is old he will not depart from it" (**Proverbs 22:6 KJV**)

Just like Lois and Eunice taught Timothy the way of the Lord, thus stirring up the gift of God in him.

"When I call to remembrance the unfeigned faith that is in thee, which dwelt first in thy grandmother Lois and thy

mother Eunice and I am persuaded that in thee also" (**2 Timothy 1:5 KJV**)

My mum embedded the Word of God early in her children and that is the only thing that has kept me so far assuring me that one day all this too will be in the past.

In the journey of life we will be beaten up, bruised, rejected, disgraced, betrayed by loved ones, blackmailed, struck down and even forsaken. However, our ability to recognize and acknowledge that our future desires and destiny can never be aborted as long as we trust God sincerely without any form of doubt or unbelief usually keep us going.

The path to our God's given destiny will have different challenges and in other to actualize destiny we need to be prepared and equipped to face them.

In **Proverbs 27:12** Solomon wrote *"the prudent see danger and take refuge but the simple keep going and pay the penalty."*

The road to success has many potholes but each experience will make the wise stronger and give better insight to overcoming its repetition.

God knew we will face so many challenges that is why He made His grace available to us. The Bible recorded the failures of great men like Moses, Elijah, Peter and Abraham to give us hope that irrespective of what we face through life's journey that our Almighty God is able to see us through it all.

So when things go wrong and the road you are trudging seems rough, when smiles gradually fades from your face and your heart beats faster for fear of the unknown, when your funds are low and your expenses are on the increase, don't give up because He that created you is well able to restore all things.

Jesus Christ experienced many challenges on His journey of reconciling man to God but he never abandoned his purpose in life. Remember God's promise never fails.

"He gives strength to the weary and increases the power of the weak" (**Isaiah 40:29 NIV**)

God's desire is for us to look unto Him and know that He never abandons His own even in the darkest moment of our lives our help will always come from Him.

We do not have to give up on ourselves! We can afford to give up on God. God cannot and will never abandon us.

Are you weary or weak? Are you looking for help? Look unto Jehovah, Our God; He is The Heaven and Earth. You can be bold as the Psalmist and declare these life-giving words.

Psalm 121 (NIV) *"I lift up my eyes to the mountains, where does my help come from? My help comes from the Lord, the maker of heaven and earth. He will not let your foot slip; he who watches over you will not slumber; indeed, he who watches over Israel will neither sleep nor slumber. The Lord watches over you, the Lord is your* *shade at your right hand; the sun will not harm you by day or the moon by night. The Lord will keep you from all harm, he will watch over your life; the Lord will watch over your coming and going both now and forevermore."*

You can also read this portion of the Bible from The Message Translation and boldly say, *"I look up to the mountains; does my strength come from mountains? No, my strength comes from God, who made heaven, and earth, and mountains. He won't let you stumble; your Guardian God won't fall asleep. Not on your life! Israel's guardian will never doze or sleep. GOD's your Guardian, right at your side to protect you- Shielding you from sunstroke, sheltering you from moonstroke. GOD guards you from every evil; he guards your very life. He guards you when you leave and when you return, he guards you now, he guards you always."* **(Psalm 121 MSG)**

This particular Psalm assures us of God's help in times of need. God wants us to totally depend on him at all times and in all things. He wants us to reject all the negative thoughts and circumstances that are trying to dominate our lives and focus on Him- Our Ever Present Help.

As you journey through life the Almighty God and the Lifter of your head will never leave nor forsake you once you are in right standing with Him.

CHAPTER TWO
LIFE AS A DREAM

Dreams are the goals and visions that fire your heart and saturate your heart with joy at the very thought of them.

They are those continuing visions of what you want your life to be at its level of highest fulfilment, what you want to do, how you want to do it, and the kind of person you want to become in the process.

Your dream draws you; it's like a magnet that pulls you towards itself. Life without a dream is like a treasure thrown into the river. Your destiny and reason for living are wrapped tightly in your dreams.

Dr. Myles Munroe wrote in his book, The Principles and Power of Vision *"that the poorest person in the world is a person without a dream."*

Your dreams and vision must be in line with God's divine plan for you because He is the source of it.

"For without me ye can do nothing..." (**John 15:5c KJV**)

At one stage in life, people have glorious dreams about their future, and try so much to bring it through but along the way, they lose focus and are distracted due to unfortunate happenings.

They end up grappling in the dark thus leaving them with the tendency to give up on their dreams and settle for just anything that comes around.

The route to your dreams may have been rocky, steep, deep, narrow and difficult, with every bend more challenging than the last; however aligning your dreams, visions, purpose to the plan and will of God is great gain. It is the heartbeat of God that His children prosper.

"Beloved I wish above all things that thou mayest prosper and be in health even as thy soul prospereth." (**3 John 1:2 KJV**)

Prosperity is the will of God for you as His beloved child, God wants every of his children to be outstanding in all aspect of life. He wants you to yield forth fruits in due season, God is able to cause that which He has spoken to come to fulfilment.

In **Genesis 37:5**, *"And joseph dreamed a dream and he told his brethren: and they hated him yet the more."*

Joseph saw a picture of his destiny, beloved your dreams firmly decides your destiny, they form the backbone of your existence.

Joseph's dreams cost him a lot, He was hated by his own brothers, *"not outsiders."* He was sold into slavery, imprisoned and forgotten but his absolute trust in God regardless of what he faced showcased Joseph and made him to be celebrated at the end.

Persistence in the place of prayer, faith and total trust in God differentiates one whose dreams and visions align with the will of God and sustains such individual in the midst of delay, stagnation, suffering, and storms of life.

As a child I had beautiful and great pictures of my world painted and wrapped up within me, even in the midst of physical, emotional and verbal abuse I was determined never to let go.

My biological father told me that I will amount to nothing; he told me I will never succeed in life! Because I constantly challenged and stood up to him for abusing my mom, his words hurt me badly and constantly echo in my ears, but on the other hand, those words made me stronger and I was determined to make it in life if not for anything to prove him wrong.

Daily I drew my strength from the Living Water - Jesus because I know that: *"Every good and perfect gift is from above coming down from the father of heavenly lights who does not change light shifting shadows"* **(James 1:17 NIV)**

A certain man in the Bible named Abraham, got married like every other man of his age, believing to bear children that he will call his own as soon as possible. He may have agreed with the wife (*Sarah*) on the number of children they would have, but things didn't go as they wished. They faced lots of unbearable and painful challenges. They became the object of discussion in the land, they were mocked by their friends and neighbours, and it seemed as if their heavens were clouded with thorns.

Frustration, heartache and depression set in for Sarah and as they grew old they wondered what will become of their lineage, I believe he asked God a million questions concerning His promises to him.

In the midst of this, the wife brought forth a suggestion and Abraham agreed!! They drifted from the will and plan of God concerning them, the natural man set in and gave them a thousand and one reasons why they should help themselves out.

Our dreams in life will be tested, tried and evaluated; it is only our ability to hope and depend on God totally that will bring fulfilment our way.

"Therefore we do not give up even though our outer person is being destroyed, our inner person is being renewed day by day" (**2nd Corinthians 4:16 HCSB**)

Let your dream be the propelling force that will navigate you to your destiny, don't lose it and never give up for your trust will be rewarded.

"Therefore let us not be weary in doing good, for at the proper time we will reap a harvest if we do not give up." (**Galatians 6:9 NIV**)

According to Dr. Mike Murdock, *"Your dream requires all of you and can be achieved by the price you are willing to pay, let your dream become your obsession and let it be the compass that directs your ship."*

Behind every story of success there are times of pain, frustration and constant dismay, Paul narrated the story of his success in **2nd Corinthians 11:23-28.**

2nd Corinthians 11:23-28 (NIV) *"...I have worked much harder, been in prison more frequently, been flogged more severely, and been exposed to death again and again. Five times I receive from the Jews forty lashes minus one. Three times I was beaten with rods, once I was stoned, three times I was shipwrecked, I spent a night and a day in the open sea, and I have been constantly on the move. I have been in danger from rivers, in danger from bandits, in danger from my own countrymen, in danger from the Gentiles, in danger in the city, in danger in the country, in danger at sea; and in danger from false brothers. I have labored and toiled and have often gone without sleep; I have known hunger and thirst and have often gone without food; I have been cold and naked. Beside everything else, I face daily the pressure of my concern for all the churches."*

There is a price to pay for every God given dream, the greater the price you pay the greater the joy you feel when you finally achieve your dream.

Dr John Maxwell wrote in his book *"Put Your Dream to Test"* that going after a dream is like climbing a mountain.

Have you abandoned your dreams and visions to discouragement, disillusionment, failure and frustration?

Let your dreams become God's will in your life, not your wishes.

"But as for you be strong and do not give up, for your work will be rewarded." (**2nd Chronicles 15:17 NIV**)

God has spoken specific things concerning you, those words are his will for your life, and you must believe them, protect them and never allow your God's given words to be aborted.

Your God's given vision must be independent of outside support or in agreement with the natural law of man. People shouldn't determine your vision for you because its actualization is in God's hands not man. He is the Master Planner, the covenant keeping God who never abandons His project.

"So is my word that goes out from my mouth; it will not return to me empty but will accomplish what I desire and achieve the purpose for which I sent it." (**Isaiah 55: 11 NIV**)

This is all the validation you need to fulfil your vision, don't spend time labouring in a vision that God has neither called nor equipped you to pursue.

Identify the source of your vision and anchor solely on the source, even when it seems your vision is dying it will spring back to life once you are connected to the right source.

People who have survived difficult pasts defied the odds and held onto their vision. Nothing is impossible in this life; trust in God for He knows the thoughts He has for you. Put your trust in God and He will take care of you, *"For I know the plans I have for you," declares the LORD, "plans to prosper you and not to harm you, plans to give you hope and a future."* (**Jeremiah 29:11 NIV**)

As you have read and seen, you have a future! The future belongs to you my dear friend. There is hope for you. You can have sure expectation of the future.

God is Awesome! He has given you a future. Rely solely on the integrity, power, ability, surety of The Almighty God, the Creator of All Things. He is TOO BIG to fail. God Has called you *"A SUCCESS and YOU ARE A SUCCESS FOREVER."*

The Bible says, *"For no word from God will ever fail."* (**Luke 1:37 NIV**) Believe the Word of God for you! Believe you are a SUCCESS! Live a life God Has called you to live, *"For with God nothing shall be impossible."* (**Luke 1: 37 KJV**)

Our God is able; He can do all things when we hold unto Him without doubt. Trust in God with all your might as you take your place in this life.

CHAPTER THREE
YOUR PERSPECTIVE OF LIFE

"God has not given us a spirit of fear, but of power and of love and of sound mind." (**2 Timothy 1:7 NIV**)

In other to improve your life, you must change your perspective of life and your way of thinking. Your perspective of life determines the route and the extent you can reach. Your thoughts about yourself have to be in line with the plan and will of God for you.

How do you see yourself? Do you believe in ideas and thoughts that are destructive to your existence? Have you succumbed to living your life based on the opinions and thoughts of others? Reducing yourself to what the public thinks of you?

The truth is that you were created by God to stand tall and stand out not to blend in or move with the crowd. Joseph's perspective of life differed from that of his brothers; he saw what they couldn't see thus his brothers couldn't understand him. Job's perspective of life even in the midst of suffering differed from that of his wife, thus his wife failed to understand why he wouldn't curse God and die.

The blind man by the pool side had a positive perspective of life, thus he believed and hoped for a better tomorrow. A right perspective of life propels the desire to succeed and enables fulfilment of one's purpose.

Sometimes we are overwhelmed by the problems of life and its intense obstacles and we tend to lose our perspective of life thus drifting away from the purpose of our creation.

The truth is that every adversity that comes our way as born again Christians has a lesson to teach us. No matter how painful our experiences in life are, there is still beauty within us, the beauty is from our knowledge of the Lord Jesus Christ Who gives beauty for ashes.

You will never be fulfilled unless you're willing to pay the price that comes with it. Personal and sometimes painful sacrifices are to be made; you may have to accept the rejection, betrayal and mistreatment in other to achieve your dream in life, you may need to walk away from friends and family members that don't add value to your life.

For the believer, right thinking is a vital necessity to fulfilling destiny. Just as water is to fish, so is positive thoughts and attitude for a purposeful life.

"For as he thinketh in his in his heart so is he." **(Proverbs 23:7a KJV)**

It is possible to look at a person's attitude and know what kind of thought that is prevalent in his life. *"A man is literally what he thinks, his character being the exact sum of all his thoughts."* Right thinking begins with the words we say to ourselves not what others say to us. The most valuable opinion is the one you have about yourself.

Many years ago, my life was in a state of chaos because of my experiences in life. The obstacles, adversities, pains, heartaches and betrayal from people I trusted. I was bruised, struck down but am still standing by His grace today knowing that with God on my side my perspective of living a successful and fulfilling life will come to pass.

Sometimes God shakes us up in a hard way in other to remove us from a toxic relationship and place us where he really wants us to be.

As a child I watched my mother being beaten, battered, abused, stripped naked and covered in her own pool of blood yet without lifting a finger to fight back.

My only option was to run about the street pleading with passers-by to come to her rescue! She was abused not for stealing or living a wayward life but for accepting Jesus Christ as her personal Lord and Saviour.

At age twelve, my life took a different direction because of the negative words my father constantly said to me. He opined that I will amount to nothing because I attended church services with my mum, those constant negative words resonated daily in my subconscious mind then.

I vividly remember one night after we came back from a church programme, my father had locked us out of the house as we knocked on the door, he came out with a burning lantern because there was power outage (*electricity*) but to my greatest shock he threw the burning lantern on my mum's head and like water, blood came gushing out.

Without any remorse my father said my mum was better off dead than alive, she was rushed to the hospital by neighbours, it was a horrible sight that left me wondering if the man I called Dad was actually human, but through it all we learnt to trust in God and depend solely on Him.

After that incident I despised my Dad and defiled his instructions, and my bravado got me several severe beatings. I endured everything because I knew all will be well someday. I encouraged myself with the Word of God that my Mum daily loaded us with.

"Thy word is a lamp unto my feet and a light unto my path." (**Psalm 119:105 KJV**)

The choice you make in life is totally yours whether to succeed in life against all odds or to lose hope and live a life of mediocrity.

When the battle of life becomes too difficult, that is when we need to depend on the strength that comes only from God knowing that He gives beauty for ashes.

"I call heaven and earth to record this day against you, that I have set before you life and death, blessing and cursing, therefore choose life that both thou and thy seed may live." (**Deuteronomy 30:19 KJV**)

CHAPTER FOUR
POWER OF CONFESSION

"FOR out of the abundance of the heart the mouth speaketh." (**Matthew 12:34b KJV**)

Our thoughts become our words and our words we confess. Therefore it is important that we choose and speak life generating words. Our daily confession should be in line with what God says about us.

Setting a guard over our mouth is very important when we speak for we will ultimately receive the things that we speak of.

"A man's belly shall be satisfied with the fruit of his mouth, and with the increase of his lips shall he be filled." (**Proverbs 18:20 KJV**)

If you are going to be what you see in your mind, and what God desires for you, your confession in the midst of adversities matters a lot. Successful men and women who impacted their generations had great thoughts, expected great things, believed great things and confessed greatness.

Words are like seeds planted into our lives and bring forth their fruit in due season. What are you sowing into your life? Your words can either make you or destroy you, it's better to sow God`s kind of words that are imperishable and uplifting.

Many years ago, I was extremely negative due to the disappointment and devastating experiences I had suffered. I was afraid to either believe or hope for anything good to come my way.

My confession gradually moved from positive to negative as I was gripped by fear of the unknown. I often wondered why God allowed me to be raised in such a dysfunctional family, with such a father that treats his children like thrash. My life moved in an unpleasant direction with those questions seeking for answers that were far-fetched; at a point I began to see myself as a problem.

Why must I struggle to achieve things that others will achieve without much effort? I prayed all manner of prayers including the prayer of Jabez, yet it seemed things were getting worse. Praying with doubt is like pouring water on the rock.

But the sequence of events occurring in my life and family pushed me deeper to search the Scriptures. When I began to study the Word and positively applied the Word of God, I let negativity go and asked God to build up a faith that will supercede the fears in me.

I have had beautiful prophesies concerning me, yet the reality was contrary to what I heard; words have the power to build up and to destroy.

I developed the attitude of saying positive things to my life, my generation; my existence and everything around me began to change. It is not what others say to you that determines your future: it's what you say to yourself when others are done speaking!

"The tongue has the power of life and death, and those who love it will eat it`s fruits" (**Proverbs 18:21**)

Let's look at the account of Caleb and the spies in **Number 13**. In this chapter the twelve spies were sent out by Moses, as we recall ten of them returned with a negative confession, they stated that taking the land was beyond their ability, *"But the men that went up with him said, We be not able to go up against the people; for they are stronger than we."* (**Number 13:31**)

Joshua and Caleb reported just the opposite, Caleb quieted the people before Moses and said to them, *"let us go up and occupy it for we are able to overcome it."* Caleb confessed out the promise of God to the Israelites in **Genesis 17:8 (ASV)** *"And I will give unto thee, and to thy seed after thee, the land of thy* *sojournings, all the land of Canaan, for an everlasting possession; and I will be their God."*

We are today's Israelites and should be faithful followers of God and prepare to face adversity by standing firm on God's word and promises.

Caleb inherited God's promises by faith, He never faltered in his confidence concerning God's ability to fulfil His promise. The obstacles, giants, distractions never stopped Caleb; don't let any situation stop you from confessing God's words and winning the battle of life.

"Say unto them, as truly as I live saith the lord, as ye have spoken in mine ears so will I do to you." (**Numbers 14:28 KJV**)

Your authority as a believer is in your mouth, God always use His words to bring about change, and you can use your words to recreate your world to your taste. No matter how negative your confession has been you can change it, I did it so you can do it too!

"Surely your goodness and mercy will follow me all the day of my life and I will dwell in the house of the lord forever" (**Psalm 23:6 NIV**)

"I shall be like a tree planted by the rivers of water that bringeth forth his fruit in his season, his leaf also shall not wither and whatsoever he doeth shall prosper" (**Psalm 1:3 KJV**)

The words you speak to yourself become self-fulfilling prophecies. Until you replace your negative self-talk with positive and faith-filled words you will always live in a state of self-denial and life full of fear.

By changing your thoughts you will begin to change your life and your world. The words you speak and listen to will build you up or pull you down, they will increase your faith or decrease it.

Our words have creative power because we are created in God's image and we have the indwelling of His power in us.

Life is always impacted to our utterances be it negative or positive words for whatever we sow, we shall reap thereof.

When you confess lack, you will experience lack in all areas of your life, you cannot talk of defeat and expect victory neither can you talk of poverty and become rich, you are replica of your confession.

Even when you are in a difficult situation don't use your words to describe the situation rather use God's Word and promises to change the situation.

Life is being given to your faith by what you say and your faith in turn brings good works. No condition is permanent no situation is irreversible.

No matter how long you have dwelt in it, God can turn things around to your favour and cause you to recover all the years that the cankerworms and palmerworms have eaten.

The reason why many of us fail to see God's promises manifest in our lives is that we see with the physical eyes, thus our spiritual eyes are blinded. With things this way, we can't see the handwriting of Jehovah on the wall concerning u; when our spiritual eyes are clouded we give in to discouragement too soon and start confessing words that aren't meant for us.

God is faithful to His words and all His promises are *"yes"* and *"amen."* As such when you confess and believe His words, not letting your emotions, mind and situations determine your confession; God in due season and at the right time will bring the words to fruition.

Hebrews 13:5c *"...for he hath said, I will never leave thee, nor forsake thee."*

God said He will never leave thee nor forsake thee, meaning that He will never fail nor leave you without support. God is saying to you, "all will be well, everything will work out fine for you because I'm in complete control of your life".

Our confessions are life and form the important aspect of our existence. I grew up in the Scripture Union family where we were thought and loaded up with Bible verses that we recite daily, though they made little or no sense to me then; but declaring them along with the family during the morning devotion and night prayers formed a vital part of my life.

I could vividly remember my favourite...**Psalm 23:1** *"The Lord is my shepherd, I shall not want"*, and **Philippians 4:19** *"but my God shall supply all my needs according to His riches in glory by Christ Jesus"* my understanding of these words then were limited as I depended solely on my parents to provide for me, so why bother myself worrying over what I need, as

I came of age, it dawned on me that all I ever needed and desired will only come through one source God! **Psalm 118:17** is one of my favourites as well.

Psalm 118:17 *"I shall not die but live and declare the works of the Lord."*

In production your input equals the output, in other words you manifest what is inside of you when encompassed with situations that are unbearable.

I was involved in a ghastly car accident on the *15th* day of February *2007*. At the point of the accident I was assumed to be dead but had to been taken to the hospital for certification.

I was told that on the way to the hospital I was murmuring some words which the doctor and the people taking me to the hospital couldn't understand but was able to write it down.

I was unconscious of my physical environment but conscious of the Word of God that has formed its root in me, unknown to me I was declaring **Psalm 118:17**, the right word and key needed at that time, it was at the point of my confession that I sneezed and came back to life.

There is power in the Word of God, there is power in our confession, your confessions and declarations are powerful tools in your hands when applied wisely in your daily living.

The doctors gave me a negative prognosis of my recovery and possible physical deformity but they were all surprise at my recovery and how God turned their human prognosis to foolishness.

In my place of worship we have a confession that we declare every Sunday service, personally I apply the confession on a daily basis and I have been greatly blessed.

This confession empowers me, strengthens me when I'm down and gives me hope in time of despair.

Please find the confession below:

I praise God for this new day, the day the Lord has made, therefore I will rejoice and be glad in it, I confess I am a new creation; the old things in my life have passed away. God is doing a new thing in my life. He will fulfil His purpose concerning me. His plans for me shall succeed. It is a new day, no confusion but new direction, no destruction but blood protection. I have parted with the failures of the past, new things are happening in my life. I confess today situations will favour me, circumstances will aid me. I declare today my paths are ordered by the Lord. I am a winner, I am more than conqueror. Mountains are levelled before me, I receive heavens dew and the earth's riches. I receive the miracle of rising up, lifting up and of sitting in the high places. I am like a tree planted by the river side. I yield my fruit in season. I am fruitful and not withered. I am prospering in all I do. Satan will not rule over me, sin will not have power over me. I am not oppressed, I am not obsessed, I am not depressed, and I am not possessed. I am not suppressed, I am not repressed, and I am not regressed. I am covered by the blood of the lamb. I confess, I declare, I believe, new beginnings, fresh anointing, new hope and great ending in Jesus name...Amen

There is life changing transformation via this confession. Declare greatness and live life without limits, it's your God given promise, confess it and possess it.

CHAPTER FIVE
THE PROPELLING FORCE

"This book of law shall not depart from your mouth, but you shall mediate on it day and night, so that you may be careful to do according to all that is written in it, for then you will make your way prosperous and then you will have good success." (**Joshua 1:8 KJV**)

God's plan for a successful life begins with keeping God's word in your mouth; According to the verse above we were reminded about the importance of the book of law not departing from our mouth.

This implies that success can only be achieved when we consistently speak words that are aligned with the Word of God. When you mediate on God's Word, it becomes an internal compass helping you determine and take charge of your life.

"Seven times a day I praise you or your righteous laws, great peace have they who love your law and nothing can make them stumble" (**Psalm 119:164-165**)

The Word of God is the propelling force towards success; it fills your heart and mind with peace and calmness in the midst of difficulties.

Whatever that will transcend to success in your life will come from direct influence of God's Words in your life. It is therefore your primary prerogative to allow God's Word to richly dwell in you, God`s Word makes you triumphant in all situations.

"For with God nothing shall be impossible" (**Luke 1:37 KJV**)

Let's look at the story of Lazarus in **John 11:1-45** *"Now a certain man was sick, named Lazarus, of Bethany, the town of Mary and her sister Martha. (It was that Mary which anointed the Lord with ointment, and wiped his feet with her hair, whose brother Lazarus was sick.) Therefore his sisters sent unto him, saying, Lord, behold, he whom thou lovest is sick. When Jesus heard that, he said, This sickness is not unto death, but for the glory of God, that the Son of God might be glorified thereby. Now Jesus loved Martha, and her sister, and*

Lazarus. When he had heard therefore that he was sick, he abode two days still in the same place where he was. Then after that saith he to his disciples, Let us go into Judaea again. His disciples say unto him, Master, the Jews of late sought to stone thee; and goest thou thither again? Jesus answered, Are there not twelve hours in the day? If any man walk in the day, he stumbleth not, because he seeth the light of this world. But if a man walk in the night, he stumbleth, because there is no light in him. These things said he: and after that he saith unto them, Our friend Lazarus sleepeth; but I go, that I may awake him out of sleep. Then said his disciples, Lord, if he sleep, he shall do well. Howbeit Jesus spake of his death: but they thought that he had spoken of taking of rest in sleep. Then said Jesus unto them plainly, Lazarus is dead. And I am glad for your sakes that I was not there, to the intent ye may believe; nevertheless let us go unto him. Then said Thomas, which is called Didymus, unto his fellow disciples, Let us also go, that we may die with him. Then when Jesus came, he found that he had lain in the grave four days already. Now Bethany was nigh unto

Jerusalem, about fifteen furlongs off: And many of the Jews came to Martha and Mary, to comfort them concerning their brother. Then Martha, as soon as she heard that Jesus was coming, went and met him: but Mary sat still in the house. Then said Martha unto Jesus, Lord, if thou hadst been here, my brother had not died. But I know, that even now, whatsoever thou wilt ask of God, God will give it thee. Jesus saith unto her, Thy brother shall rise again. Martha saith unto him, I know that he shall rise again in the resurrection at the last day. Jesus said unto her, I am the resurrection, and the life: he that believeth in me, though he were dead, yet shall he live: And whosoever liveth and believeth in me shall never die. Believest thou this? She saith unto him, Yea, Lord: I believe that thou art the Christ, the Son of God, which should come into the world. And when she had so said, she went her way, and called Mary her sister secretly, saying, The Master is come, and calleth for thee. As soon as she heard that, she arose quickly, and came unto him. Now Jesus was not yet come into the town, but was in that place where Martha met him. The Jews then which were with her in the house, and comforted her, when they saw Mary, that she rose up hastily and went out, followed her, saying, She goeth unto the grave to weep there. Then when Mary was come where Jesus was, and saw him, she fell down at his feet, saying unto him, Lord, if thou hadst been here, my brother had not died. When Jesus therefore saw her weeping, and the Jews also weeping which came with her, he groaned in the spirit, and was troubled. And said, Where have ye laid him? They said unto him, Lord, come and see. Jesus wept. Then said the Jews, Behold how he loved him! And some of them said, Could not this man, which opened the eyes of the blind, have caused that even this man should not have died? Jesus therefore again groaning in himself cometh to the grave. It was a cave, and a stone lay upon it. Jesus said, Take ye away the stone. Martha, the sister of him that was dead, saith unto him, Lord, by this time he stinketh: for he hath been dead four days. Jesus saith unto her, Said I not unto thee, that, if thou wouldest believe, thou shouldest see the glory of God? Then they took away the stone from the place where the dead was laid. And Jesus lifted up his eyes, and said,

Father, I thank thee that thou hast heard me. And I knew that thou hearest me always: but because of the people which stand by I said it, that they may believe that thou hast sent me. And when he thus had spoken, he cried with a loud voice, Lazarus, come forth. And he that was dead came forth, bound hand and foot with grave clothes: and his face was bound about with a napkin. Jesus saith unto them, Loose him, and let him go. Then many of the Jews which came to Mary, and had seen the things which Jesus did, believed on him."

Lazarus's sisters sent message to Jesus when he was sick but instead of coming immediately, Jesus waited for extra two days, when He eventually arrived, Lazarus had been dead and buried for four days.

But Jesus said in **John 11:11** that His friend Lazarus *"sleepeth"* and that He is going to wake him up from sleep, even the disciples didn't understand what their Master said.

The beauty of this account is that there is no impossibility with God, Jesus gives hope to the hopeless and beautifies every ugly situation.

Martha and Mary blamed Jesus for their brother's death yet believed that with God nothing is impossible and Jesus assured them that their brother will live again.

The Bible recorded in **John 11:35** that *"Jesus wept."* As Jesus Christ wept when He saw Lazarus where he laid so He weeps for you today in that situation you are hemmed in. Our Lord and Saviour Jesus Christ does not delight in seeing you in pain. Whatever pain you are passing through, Jesus feels your pain and He is at your door, ready to heal you.

Are you in any difficult situation? Do you feel God is delaying the answers to your prayers? Do you trust God even in that delay? Remember, if He can raise Lazarus from death, He can do the impossible.

God's Word prepares us for any situation, when you daily load yourself with the word of God nothing takes you by surprise. It is only then you will understand there are some battles you are fighting that has already been won by our Lord Jesus. In essence, all you need do is to consistently stand in the victory that Jesus has given you.

"for as the rain cometh down and the snow from heaven, and returneth not thither but watereth the earth and maketh it bring forth and bud, that it may give seed to the sower and bread to the eater: so shall my word be that goeth forth out of my mouth: it shall not return unto me void but it shall accomplish that which I please and it shall prosper in the thing whereto I sent it" (**Isaiah 55:10-11 KJV**)

When I realized the potency of the Word of God, I daily applied it to my life, it changed everything around me. God's promises replaced every negative occurrence and thought coming from within and outside.

Mark 5:35-43 *"While he yet spake, there came from the ruler of the synagogue's house certain which said, Thy* *daughter is dead: why troublest thou the Master any further? As soon as Jesus heard the word that was spoken, he saith unto the ruler of the synagogue, Be not afraid, only believe. And he suffered no man to follow him, save Peter, and James, and John the brother of James. And he cometh to the house of the ruler of the synagogue, and seeth the tumult, and them that wept and wailed greatly. And when he was come in, he saith unto them, Why make ye this ado, and weep? the damsel is not dead, but sleepeth. And they laughed him to scorn. But when he had put them all out, he taketh the father and the mother of the damsel, and them that were with him, and entereth in where the damsel was lying. And he took the damsel by the hand, and said unto her, Talitha cumi; which is, being interpreted, Damsel, I say unto thee, arise. And straightway the damsel arose, and walked; for she was of the age of twelve years. And they were astonished with a great astonishment. And he charged them straitly that no man should know it; and commanded that something should be given her to eat."*

In the scripture above, while Jesus was still speaking some people came from the house of Jairus the synagogue ruler; "your daughter is dead" they said why bother Jesus the Teacher anymore but Jesus didn't listen to them, He told Jairus not to be afraid but believe.

I assume that was a very crucial moment in the life of Jairus; he may have been wondering whose report to believe. Should he believe the report of his people that his daughter was dead or trust Jesus for the power of resurrection!

Jesus went to Jairus house with Peter, James and John. There were confusions everywhere, people crying and sobbing loudly. Jesus went inside and said to them the child is not dead, she is only *"sleeping"* but they laughed at him.

Are you going through stuffs? Are people and situations laughing at you? Do your friends and family members question you potency of your God? Relax and lift your head up because you will laugh the best laugh and dance like never before for He that is working on your behalf can neither fail nor abandon a project that He started. You are a pencil in God's hands...clay that He is refining into a masterpiece...

Jesus made them all go outside, He took only the child's father, mother and the disciples who were with Him and went in where the child laid. Jesus took her by the hand and said *"Talitha cumi"* meaning "little girl I say to you get up!" Right away she stood up and walked around, they were totally amazed at this, then Jesus asked them to give her something to eat.

Jesus will take your mockers by surprise and turn your misery to miracles. Jairus was helpless and hopeless till he met Jesus, Who restored life to a lifeless body and turned the adverse situations around.

Jesus is always right on time, trust and depend on Him totally. He will show forth sooner than you think because it's your time to shine.

Here are scriptures that will strengthen you in times of despair.

"No weapon formed against you shall prosper, and every tongue which raises against you in judgment you shall condemn, this is the heritage of the servants of the lord, and their righteousness is from me." **(Isaiah 54:17 KJV)**

"For in the day of trouble he will keep me safe in his dwellings, he will hide me in the shelter of his tabernacle and set me high upon a rock." **(Psalm 27:5 NIV)**

"And the lord shall make thee the head, and not the tail and thou shalt be above only and thou shalt not be beneath, if that thou hearken unto the commandments of the lord thy God which I command you this day to observe and to do them." **(Deuteronomy 28:13 KJV)**

"For our present trouble are small and won't last very long. Yet they produce for us a glory that vastly outweighs them and will last forever." **(2nd Corinthians 4:17 NLT)**

"Yea though I walk through the valley of the shadow of death, I will fear no evil, for thou art with me, thy rod and thy staff they comfort me." (**Psalm 23:4 KJV**)

"Don't be afraid for I am with you, do not be dismayed for I am your God, I will strengthen you, I will help you, I will uphold you with my victorious right hand." (**Isaiah 41:10 NLT**)

"We are hard pressed on every side, but not crushed, perplexed but not in despair, persecuted but not abandoned, struck down but not destroyed." (**2nd Corinthians 4:8-9 NIV**)

"The Lord is close to the broken hearted, He rescues those whose spirit are crush." (**Psalm 34:18 NLT**)

CHAPTER SIX
FLEE AT ALL COST

Vines an expository dictionary of New Testament words partially defines *"DOUBT"* in the verb form as to stand in two ways implying uncertainty.

The Oxford English Dictionary defines DOUBT, in the noun form as a feeling of uncertainty or lack of conviction. Doubt and unbelief are often assumed to mean the same thing but the two are very different, both are powerful tools of the enemy that believers must flee from at all cost.

According to the oxford dictionary unbelief is lack of religious belief, an absence of faith. Doubt is of the heart and it manifests in action or inaction, decision or indecision.

Doubt or unbelief is the opposite of faith. God gave us the measure of faith but the devil tries to negate our faith by attacking us with doubt thus opposing the word of God in our lives.

"For by the grace given me I say to every one of you, do not think of yourself more highly than you ought, but rather think of yourself with sober judgment in accordance with the faith God has distributed to each of you." **(Romans 12:3 NIV)**

Doubt hinders the blessings of God and makes it impossible for us to please God **(*Hebrews 11:6a*)** *"for without faith it is impossible to please God"*. Doubt causes an individual to miss the plan and provision of God for his or her life.

Doubt makes one vulnerable to believing the report of the enemy instead of believing God. Doubt satisfies our need for self-protection because our subconscious reasoning says it's easier not to trust than to be disappointed. Doubt sets in gradually and completely takes over when we fail to combat it with the word of God.

"Faith cometh by hearing and hearing by the word of God." **(Romans 10:17 KJV)**

Faith is the only means by which we enter into the perfect will of God for our lives. It is the spiritual force that propels victory in a believer's journey to excel.

Doubt is contagious, **Proverbs 6:2** *"Thou art snared with the words of thy mouth, thou art taken with the words of thy mouth."*

It matters how you speak and the words you speak! Your faith-filled words, backed by great faith-filled actions can transform your life and inspire you to be the very best.

Let us consider the account of the woman with the issue of blood who demonstrated her faith in action.

Luke 8:43-48 *"And a woman having an issue of blood twelve years, which had spent all her living upon physicians, neither could be healed of any, Came behind him, and touched the border of his garment: and immediately her issue of blood stanched. And Jesus said, Who touched me? When all denied, Peter and they that were with him said, Master, the multitude throng thee* *and press thee, and sayest thou, Who touched me? And Jesus said, Somebody hath touched me: for I perceive that virtue is gone out of me. And when the woman saw that she was not hid, she came trembling, and falling down before him, she declared unto him before all the people for what cause she had touched him, and how she was healed immediately. And he said unto her, Daughter, be of good comfort: thy faith hath made thee whole; go in peace."*

This nameless woman has visited so many physicians in search of a cure for her haemorrhagic condition; she had suffered for twelve years.

She was very wealthy so she visited the best physicians in town but all to no avail, the reports from the doctors were negative, hopeless and dreadful.

She had every reason to be depressed and even take her life because she was considered unclean according to Jewish law, *"And the priest shall offer the one for a sin offering, and the other for a burnt offering; and the priest shall make an atonement for her before the*

LORD for the issue of her uncleanness." (**Leviticus 15:30**)

Anything she touches also becomes contaminated and unclean. This woman made a choice, she disregarded the stigma that is attached to her condition and sought Jesus, and she broke the law, neglected her circumstances and believed without doubt that if she could only touch the hem of His garment (*Jesus*) she will be made *"whole."*

Traditionally, this woman made Jesus unclean by touching the hem of His garment, but her total faith without doubt restored her. The woman fell down trembling but Jesus comforted her and told her that her *"FAITH"* has made her whole!

It was faith that made her whole not her money or connections. When you allow the seed of doubt and unbelief to dwell in you, you are just denying the existence of God in your life and believing the lies of the enemy. Everything is possible and achievable through Jesus Christ.

"But let him ask in faith, not wavering. For he that wavereth is like a wave of the sea driven with the wind and tossed." (**James 1:6 KJV**)

A doubting mind cannot receive anything from the Lord because God hides his face from such a person.

"And he said I will hide my face from them; I will see what their end shall be: for they are a very forward generation, children in whom is no faith."
(**Deuteronomy 32:20 KJV**)

Doubt sinks a man in the storms of life; it renders a man fearful at all times and makes the person a victim instead of a victor.

"And peter answered him and said, Lord if it be thou, bid me come unto thee on the water, and he said, come. And when peter was come down out of the ship, he walked on water to go to Jesus. But when he saw the wind boisterous he was afraid; and beginning to sink, he cried, saying lord save me" (**Matthew 14:28-30**)

God places dreams and visions in the hearts of His people. Don't let the boisterous wind of discouragement, obstacles, delay, and dissentient circumstances cause you to abort your God given dreams.

Don't let the enemy steal your seed, he doesn't want you to get your mind in agreement with our God given spirit. Satan is only interested in abolishing God's plan for your life, do not aid him by allowing unbelief and doubt to occupy the better part of you.

"The thief cometh not, but for to steal, and to kill and to destroy" (**John 10:10 KJV**)

Against all odds, Abraham hoped and believed God to fulfil His promise concerning him. Without wavering in his faith, he refused the fact that his body was as good as dead since he was about an hundred years old and that Sarah's womb was also dead, yet he did not waver through unbelief regarding the promises of God. He was strengthened in his faith and gave glory to God, being fully persuaded that God had power to do what He had promised.

God promised Abraham an heir from his own loins, many years passed yet the promise remained unfulfilled. He was attacked by doubt and unbelief, but he continued to be steadfast giving glory to God in his period of waiting. He believed and received. The woman with the issue of blood believed and received as well, the blind man by the pool side believed and received too! You can only receive when you believe. Faith is what Satan hates the most and it is what God demands most from us. Faith is the fundamental element to achieving success in life.

"Now in the morning, as he returned in the city he was hungry and seeing a fig tree by the road he came to it and found nothing on it but leaves, and said to it "let no fruit grow on you ever again" immediately the fig tree withered away. And when the disciples saw it, they marveled,

saying how did the fig tree wither away so soon? So Jesus answered and said to them "assuredly, I say to you if you have faith and do not doubt, you will not only do what was done to the fig tree, but also if you say to this mountain, be removed and be cast into the sea, it will be done. And whatever thing you ask in prayer believing you will receive." (**Matthew 21:18-22 NKJV**)

Faith is a gift from God, "*...according as God hath dealt to every man the measure of faith*" (**Romans 12:3**) but doubt is a choice. You have the will power to reject it when the enemy projects the undesirable situations above the power of God. Unbelief leads to disobedience and will keep you from fulfilling what God has designed you to accomplish in life.

"For let not that man suppose that he will receive anything from the lord, he is a double minded man, unstable in all his ways." (**James 1:7-8 NKJV**)

Trust God in all your ways because He that has called you is able to accomplish all that concerns you. Learn to live from faith to faith, it is the only way to overcome, don't let the devil steal your future from you through lies, you are God's masterpiece, don't live in fear!

CHAPTER SEVEN
POWER OF FORGIVENESS

Forgiveness is giving up my right to hurt you for hurting me. The word *"forgive"* means to wipe the slate clean, to pardon, to cancel a debt.

Forgiving is an act of love, mercy and grace, it is not granted because a person deserves it but because it's in accordance, in obedience and submission to God's will, trusting God to bring emotional healing. *"If you forgive those who sin against you, your heavenly father will forgive you. But if you reuse to forgive others, your father will not forgive your sins."* **(Matthew 6:14-15)**

"Let all bitterness and wrath and anger and clamor and evil speaking be put away from you with all malice; and be ye kind one to another tender hearted, forgiving one another even as God for Christ's sake hath forgiven you." **(Ephesians 4:31-32 KJV)**

As a believer we are under obligation to God to forgive our offenders as eternal destiny depends upon it. We cannot hold grudges or seek revenge when God has commanded us to forgive our transgressors.

When we forgive we release our offenders from wrongs they committed against us, leaving the event in God's hands and moving through the grace God has made available for us.

I wrestled with unforgiveness for years. I bottled up myself in bitterness, anger and pain. I gave the enemy the right to fill my mind with wrong reasons why I shouldn't forgive my offenders and let go off hurts done to me.

He ended up building thousand and one boundaries for me, enslaving me in pity and giving me reasons to protect myself from being hurt again.

For years I couldn't come to terms with my Dad, as far as I was concerned he was dead and buried in my life and constantly I backed up my life reactions and attitudes with the Bible passages that suites me.

"Do not be unequally yoked together with unbelievers. For what fellowship has righteousness with lawlessness? And what communion has light with darkness." (**2 Corinthians 6:14**)

Beloved, the enemy indeed is in the business of deceit, and he will always back his activities with Bible passages because that's the only way he will engage you in fulfilling his heart beat unknowingly.

As time passed by the list of my offenders increased drastically that I couldn't contend with it. It is impossible to live on this planet without getting hurt, offended, misunderstood, lied to, lied about and rejected.

Have you been abandoned in the hospital when you needed someone to lean on? Have you been called names by friends that you so much trusted? Have you been accused wrongly by people you hold dear to your heart? Have your name made waves in a negative way? Have your friends ganged up against you to bring you down? Have you felt the pain that only a father can help you out but he wasn't there? Have you been cursed instead of being blessed?

I was judged wrongly and my actions were wrongly judged as well. My words were given a different interpretation, my looks were misinterpreted. Though I smiled but behind that pretty smile, behind that Sunday praise was a person who was hurting and craving for revenge, my life was in turmoil.

One day the chains were broken and I heard the chains fell off. Beloved, your place of worship will determine how well you will run and end your heavenly race; it will either make you or destroy you.

What you hear is important and who you listen to is more important because you should be guided by the true undiluted word of God that is painful to do yet brings healing to the hurting soul.

Unresolved anger keeps us from moving forward, it locks us up, freezes us to that moment when the offence occurred. Fear of being hurt again bottles us up from moving to new levels of relationships not only with our offenders but with others as well. Everyone becomes a suspect at this point.

One day I heard a message on forgiveness, it wasn't my first time of listening to messages on forgiveness but there was something unique and different about the message this time.

The message was ministered by a Man of God who has yielded himself totally to God and His will. I felt the passion of the word of God in a unique way ministering directly to me and breaking every chain and walls that has bound me all these years.

I couldn't help myself but I gave in to God to remould and mend me. As if that wasn't enough a brother in my place of worship was led to encourage us through his word of testimony. He told us how God enabled him to forgive his father and family.

I thought mine was unbearable but after listening to this fellow I saw bitterness, rejection, hurt and pain in another level, it was a peculiar case but he forgave them all and treated them as family.

I sincerely prayed for God's enabling grace and He heard me. It was not an easy process because I felt cheated, inconvenienced and weak but it was a step worth taking.

From that moment on I experienced God's unquantifiable peace and joy. Things that naturally will hurt me I barely noticed, things that I will hear and get worried I lay off easily without blinking.

Unforgiving spirit is a robber that steals one's peace, joy and relationship with God and puts you on your toes always.

Forgiveness is non-negotiable; it is the very essence of our faith, and the enemy is using it as a powerful weapon to debar us from fulfilling God's commandment thereby disobeying God.

EFFECT OF UNFORGIVENESS IN OUR LIVES AS BELIEVERS...

It hinders your prayers from being answered

"Therefore I say unto you what things so ever ye desire, when ye pray, believe that ye receive them and ye shall have them. And when ye stand praying, forgive, if ye have ought against any; that your father also which is in heaven may forgive you your trespasses." **(Mark 11: 24-25 KJV)**

Unforgiveness defiles a believer

"Follow peace with all men, and holiness, without which no man shall see the lord; looking diligently lest any man fail of the grace of God; lest any root of bitterness springing up trouble you and thereby many be defile" **(Hebrew 12:14-15 KJV)**

Unforgiveness inhibits you from living life without limits

When you fail to forgive, you won't enter into His presence with boldness, the devil who is the accuser of the brethren will always remind you of those who offended you; those you have refused to forgive.

The devil will give you thousand and one reasons why God will not bless you since you are disobeying His command; *"and shall come to pass, if thou shalt hearken diligently unto the voice of the lord thy God, to observe and do all his commandment which I command thee this day, that the lord thy God will set thee on high above all nations of the earth; and all these blessings shall come on thee and overtake thee, if thou shall hearken unto the voice of the lord thy God; blessed shall thou be in the city, and blessed shall thou be in the field"* **(Deuteronomy 28:1-3 KJV)**

You bear no spiritual fruit with unforgiveness residing in you

"But the fruit of the spirit is love, joy, peace, longsuffering, gentleness, goodness, faith, meekness, temperance; against such there is no law" (**Galatians 5:22-23 KJV**)

One that harbours bitterness, resentment, hurt and pain has no love in him. God is love, it was love that reconciled man to God and it's only through love that we can effectively function as believers and achieve the heartbeat of God which is witnessing.

The act of forgiveness is our seed of obedience to God's Word, once we obey Him; He opens the door and pours out His harvest of blessings upon us. Forgiveness opens a channel of genuine fellowship with God. It gives us the authority to rule our world and leaves no room for the enemy to take advantage of us.

"To whom ye forgive anything, I forgive also; for if I forgave anything, to whom I forgave it, for your sakes forgave I it in the person of Christ; lest Satan should get an advantage of us; for we are not ignorant of his devices."
(**2 Corinthians 2:10-11 KJV**)

When we forgive we let go and let God, **Hebrew 10: 30** says that vengeance belongs to the Lord; *"For we know him that hath said, Vengeance belongeth unto me, I will recompense, saith the Lord. And again, The Lord shall judge his people."* (**Hebrews 10:30**)

He will repay and settle the cases. If we put our offenders in God's hand through forgiveness He knows how to recompense them for the hurt, injustices and betrayal they caused us.

The Potter is also able to mend your heart and fill you up with His peace and joy that is beyond human understanding. Forgiveness is more than emotions, it is a decision you make, let go and let God!

CHAPTER EIGHT
LOOKING UNTO JESUS

"Looking unto Jesus the author and finisher of our faith."
(Hebrews 12: 29)

Without a God-given vision you will stumble through life and lose focus on your personality and what God can accomplish through you. Without God's given vision one moves around spiritually blind thus losing the concept of true life and understanding of God's promises.

A lot of things may come against you in your family, your finances or your health. Your environment may be saying words that are contrary to God's given promises but you can only overcome when you fix your eye on the Almighty God who is the Author and Finisher of our faith. When you get into agreement with God, He releases His promises and causes non-existent things to exist for you. In other to activate God's given promises you must depend solely on Him.

"For a great door and effectual is opened unto me and there are many adversaries." (**1st Corinthians 16: 9 KJV**)

What are you looking unto? What are you focusing on? The open doors or the adversaries? The opportunities or the obstacles? Jesus can help you find the treasure in your field.

"Again ,the kingdom of heaven is like unto treasure hid in a field, the which when a man hath found, he hideth, and for joy thereof goeth and selleth all that he hath, and buyeth that field" *"Again the kingdom of heaven is like a merchant seeking goodly pearls."* (**Matthew 13:44-45 KJV**)

If Jesus can turn water into wine, think of other things He can do through you, the question is what do you see? Who is your source? What are you focused on?

I remember the story of the bronze serpent made by Moses in **Numbers 21:5-9** when the Israelites complained bitterly against God, He sent poisonous snakes among the rebels.

Numbers 21:5-9 *"And the people spake against God, and against Moses, Wherefore have ye brought us up out of Egypt to die in the wilderness? For there is no bread, neither is there any water; and our soul loatheth this light bread. And the LORD sent fiery serpents among the people, and they bit the people; and much people of Israel died. Therefore the people came to Moses, and said, We have sinned for we have spoken against the LORD, and against thee; pray unto the LORD, that he take away the serpents from us. And Moses prayed for the people. And the LORD said unto Moses, Make thee a fiery serpent, and set it upon a pole: and it shall come to pass, that every one that is bitten, when he looketh upon it, shall live. And Moses made a serpent of brass, and put it upon a pole, and it came to pass, that if a serpent had bitten any man, when he beheld the serpent of brass, he lived."*

The bronze serpent was provided as a visible means for repentance and everyone that looked on the pole with the bronze serpent was cured of the snakebite.

Thus when we are encompassed with so many poisonous situations, looking unto Jesus Christ who never fails is our only hope of victory. God's word will hold you up when you go through chaotic experiences, His words brings stability in all circumstances.

No other counsel will get you through the long haul, no other truth will help you stand firm in the storms of uncertainty. No other reality will give you strength you need each day; the only way to pull through with your head held up is through our Lord Jesus Christ.

The Word of God has so much power that it is more effective than any therapy; God can illuminate a scripture that goes back into the past and heal your entire wound, give you direction in the middle of despair and provide you with hope for the future.

Beloved, nothing about you surprises God in spite of what you have been through, God hasn't changed, His concept about you and what you are destined to become stands firm.

You are on a mission and that mission you have to fulfil, that's why the enemy has tried so hard to abort your mission, make you lose focus and wander around without vision.

As you study the Word of God you will begin to experience life-changing and mind-renewing power deposited in you.

God sees the big picture; He loves you so much and wouldn't want to watch you fail in your God given assignment. When the obstacles seem too big and oppositions seem too strong, do not be afraid because He that is in you is greater and can never be defeated.

Dr. Maureen I. Austin

"Trust in the lord with all thine heart and lean not unto thine own understanding" (**Proverbs 3:5 KJV**)

CHAPTER NINE
GOD'S GRACE, YOUR GAIN

When we forgive, we liberate ourselves from the bondage of the enemy and embrace the peace of God that passes all understanding, we off load the weight on our neck that blocks our personal relationship with God.

The Word, peace is defined as the state of harmony characterized by the lack of violence, conflict behaviours and the freedom from fear of violence. Commonly understood as the absence of hostility, existence of healthy or newly healed interpersonal or international relationship, or personality free from internal and external strife. Freedom from quarrels and disagreement, harmonious relations, inner contentment and serenity.

Biblically the word peace means *"to be complete"* or "to be sound". The Hebrew word for peace is "*shalom*" which means completeness, wholeness, health, safety soundness, tranquillity, prosperity, welfare, perfectness, fullness, rest, and harmony.

Being filled with spiritual peace is to be spiritually healthy and free from all discord in the soul, it is a condition of freedom from disturbance within the soul, it is an inner sense of contentment and quietness regardless of life's circumstances, it is steadfast confidence in our heavenly father, it is the presence of joy in the midst of unhappiness.

When the peace of God is in you there will be no room for jealousy, envy, discontentment, uncontrolled temper, selfishness, pride, intolerance, harsh criticism and fear of anxiety.

I have not come across any promise in the Bible that says we will be free from troubles, wars, temptations, sorrows, tears and trials but God promised us His peace in the midst of the storm. I grew up in a home filled with turmoil; it was a very unstable and unpleasant environment, full of anger and all kinds of abuse physical, verbal and emotional abuse.

I lived with the frustrations, aggravations, worry, bitterness and the fire of revenge for years, all these negative attitudes became cancerous to my existence.

Then I read a book titled *'God's Rest in a Restless World* by a Man of God I hold in high esteem, Pastor Solomon Olu'sogo Adelaja, an epitome of God's peace manifested, he stressed that God's Word gives peace to those that love it, **Psalms 119:165** *"great peace have they which love thy law and nothing shall offend them"*.

The peace that is beyond reasoning, beyond logic, beyond earthly wisdom and knowledge, peace that is not based on material achievements, God`s kind of peace is indescribable.

In that book, the Author buttresses that this kind of peace is only possible when we acknowledge and live by **Psalm 1: 1-3** which says, *"Happy are those* *who reject the advice of evil people, who do not follow the example of sinners or join those who have no use for God. Instead, they find joy in obeying the law of the lord, and they study it day and night. They are like trees that grow beside a stream that bears fruit at the right time, and whose leaves do not dry up. They succeed in everything they do."*

It is possible to be born-again for years without experiencing God's peace.

Mark 4:37-39 *"And there arose a great storm of wind, and the waves beat into the ship, so that it was now full. And he was in the hinder part of the ship, asleep on a pillow: and they awake him, and say unto him, Master, carest thou not that we perish? And he rose, and rebuked the wind, and said unto the sea, Peace, be still. And the wind ceased, and there was a great calm."*

In the scripture above, the disciples were with Jesus Christ on a ship sailing on the Sea of Galilee, Jesus was asleep and a great storm arose. The ship took in so much water with tidal wave beating it to and fro.

The disciples became fearful, they panicked and ran to wake Jesus from sleep and said to Him *"carest thou not that we perish?"*

They were in the same ship with the Prince of Peace yet they lacked the peace of God within them. They have been with Jesus for years yet they were fearful at the storms of life.

The enemy is persistent and will do whatever he can to wear us out and keep us from God's will, but as children of the most high God we need to have the same tenacity as Christ. Decide to never give up our God's given peace.

Romans 8:37 *"Nay, in all these things we are more than conquerors through him that loved us."* This assures us that we have complete victory in all things through Christ that loved us; if we have confidence in God Almighty we shouldn't lose our sleep over any unfriendly situation knowing that we are victorious over our adversary.

Our adversary may send all kinds of life-defeating, joy-stealing attacks to threaten our well-being and faith in God. God never abandons His own, He fights our battles, and even in our darkest moments He always shows up and gives us beauty for ashes.

The Bible recorded in Daniel **6**, that the Almighty God protected Daniel in the lion's den. He was in his darkest moment but he never lost his peace, his confidence and assurance remained in God- Who in His Almightiness saved Daniel. The same God that saved Daniel and the three Hebrew men is still in the business of watching over His own, if He can watch over the sparrow, feed them, clothe them, how much more you that He made to worship Him.

God never sleeps nor slumbers, the Psalmist wrote in **Psalm 139: 7-12** *"where could I go to escape from you? Where could I get away from your presence? if I went up to heaven, you would be there, if I lay down in the world of the dead, you would be there, if I flew away beyond the east or lived in the farthest place in the west,* *you will be there to lead me, you will be there to help me. I could ask the darkness to hide me or the light round me to turn into night, but even darkness is not even dark for you and the night is as bright as the day. Darkness and light are the same to you."*

When we understand who God is to us we won't lose our peace over anything, for in the fiercest of battles, while the storm is at its peak, the trusting soul can know inward peace and tranquillity. There can be a deep down calm and quiet confidence in God.

Jesus rebuked the wind and the sea *"peace be still"*; no one else could have done that but the Lord Jesus Christ. He can speak peace to your life, He promised to be with you at all times *"when you pass through deep waters, I will be with you, your troubles will not overwhelm you, when you pass through fire you will not be burnt, the hard trials that come will not hurt you."* **(Isaiah 43:2 GNB)**

God's peace is sufficient and meets our everyday need. It guards our minds and calms our heart. It is determined by our Lord Jesus Christ who obtained it for us at the Cross. God's peace is permanent and not intermittent; it's not determined by external factors. It flows through our souls through Jesus Christ. One can never know the peace of God until one has come to peace with God.

"There is no peace, says my God for the wicked." (**Isaiah 57:21 NIV**)

The peace of God enables one to endure the avalanche of hardship and difficulty while still retaining and enjoying an inner peace. This peace surpasses all human understanding because the spirit of God lives in him. Peace is part of our inheritance in Christ.

"Peace I leave with you; my peace I give to you; not as the world gives do I give to you. Do not let your heart be troubled, nor let it be fearful." (**John 14: 27 NASB**)

CONCLUSION

Living a victorious life requires faith that can move mountains, faith that can stand the test of time against all odds.

Faith empowers us to confront our challenges and speak positively to them. The Bible says that faith without works is dead which means that praying without faith is a waste of time. Each time we speak the Word of faith something happens in the realm of the Spirit.

Faith in God is the propelling force that keeps one standing irrespective of what the situations are. Faith is the invisible mirror that lets you see things differently from other people's perceptions.

It was faith that changed Abraham's situation, faith brought healing to the woman with the issue of blood, and faith restored the sight of blind Bartimaeus. Faith kept Job in spite of his challenges, it was faith in God that gave David victory over Goliath, and faith brought Jarius daughter back to life!

Note this, there isn't any miracle in the Bible that came to fulfilment without faith and there won't be any miracle in your life without faith in God Almighty.

"Now faith is the substance of things hoped for the evidence of things not seen." (**Hebrews11:1 KJV**)

Faith is a catalyst, it makes things happen, faith makes God word work in one's life, without faith nothing happens.

The vital ingredient to understanding the word of God and applying it in our daily living is our understanding of how a tiny faith-like that of a mustard seed can move mountain and turn things around to our favour.

Life may have beaten you hardly, badly and roughly but you can still excel beyond your imaginations by trusting God's word and acting in faith. God's promises will bloom in your life once you spark off your faith in Him. He will supernaturally do for you what you could not do for yourself.

"And the lord shall make you the head and not the tail and thou shall be above only and shall not be beneath."
(Deuteronomy 28:13)

You may feel there are too many challenges between you and your God given destiny, if Christ can feed the multitudes with five loaves of bread and two fishes, He is more than able to handle that which concerns you.

When time gets tough look up to the hill where your help comes from. The only Source that can never run dry or be temporarily out of service is God. God is the only anchor that never disappoints. Stay strong and see you at the top.

GOD FAVOURED ME

(*SONG BY Hezekiah Walker*)

This is my testimony everybody,

How God favoured me in spite of my enemies and I, God did it for me

He will do the same for you.

Don't worry about your haters, for they can't do you any harm.

Love is patient, caring, love is kind,

Love is felt most when it's genuine

But I have had my share of love abused, manipulated and its strength misused

And I can't help but give you the glory,

When I think about my story

And I know you favoured me

Because my enemies did try but couldn't triumph over me,

Yes they did try but couldn't triumph over me.

I'm still here, I'm still alive, and I'm still blessed,

On my way to my destiny

Because the favour of God is on my life.

They whispered, conspired,

They told their lies (God favoured me)
My character, my integrity,
My faith in God will never fail, will not bend, won't compromise (God favoured me)
I speak life and prosperity,
I speak health (God favoured me).

NEVER WOULD HAVE MADE IT
(*BY MARVIN SAPP*)

Never would have made it,

Never would have made it without you,

I would have lost it all

But now I see how you were there for me,

And I can say never would I have made it without you,

I would have lost it all but now I see,

How you were there for me,

I'm stronger; I'm wiser, I'm better, much better. When I look back over all you brought me through, I can see that you were the One I held on to.

I would have lost it, if it had not been for you.

I made it through my storm and my test

Because you were there to carry me through my mess.

I can stand here and tell you I made it

Because I held firm on to you.

ABOUT THE AUTHOR

Dr. Maureen .I. Austin is a Certified Veterinary Doctor, Member of the Royal College of Surgeons Nigeria. She graduated from the Prestigious University of Nigeria, Nsukka Enugu State. She also holds a diploma in Adult Psychology and Social Studies from Irish Colleges. She attended the Redeemers Bible College, Republic of Ireland and serves as a Music Minister in RCCG Ireland. She is highly blessed of God.

ABOUT THE BOOK

This book is an inspirational make over to understanding, acknowledging and affirming our daily living in line with the word of God.

Struck Down But Not Destroyed is based on true life experiences and how God's grace enables us to live victoriously.

Everyone goes through challenges in life; these challenges may leave one in a state of dilemma, hardship, heartache, unforgiveness or intermittent joy and celebration.

This book will give you an insight on how to change your life by changing your word and mindset. Through the trials, tragedies and ultimate victories from the author's experience that led her to wondrous, life-transforming truth through the word of God your testimony will be born. Never give up on yourself.

The battle of life is the battle of words. Arm yourself

with the Word of God, praise and prayer. Take charge of your life and find freedom and peace. Embracing life's challenges and aiming high is what you were made for....

SEE YOU AT THE TOP!!

www.ingramcontent.com/pod-product-compliance
Lightning Source LLC
Chambersburg PA
CBHW060338050426
42449CB00011B/2787